HEADLINES OF THE CENTURY

1910-1919

Melissa Stone Billings
Henry Billings

STECK-VAUGHN
COMPANY
A Subsidiary of National Education Corporation

Books in this series:

Headlines of the Century 1910-1919

Headlines of the Century 1920-1929

Headlines of the Century 1930-1939

Headlines of the Century 1940-1949

Acknowledgments

Executive Editor
Elizabeth Strauss

Project Editor
Kelly Krake

Designer
John Harrison

Electronic Production
Shelly Knapp, Kristian Polo

Photo Editor
Margie Foster

Illustration Credits
P. 3 David Griffin

Photo Credits
Cover (inset) The Bettmann Archive; P.5 UPI/Bettmann; p.6 Culver Pictures; p.7 The Bettmann Archive; pp.11, 12 Courtesy Harvard University Archives; p.13 James Minor; p.14 (top)© Doug Armand/TSW; (bottom both) NASA; pp.19, 20, 21 Courtesy Indianapolis Motor Speedway; p.25 The Bettmann Archive; p.26 © John Lamb/TSW; pp. 27, 28 The Bettmann Archive; p.29 © Graham Harris/TSW; p.33 The Bettmann Archive; p.34 Culver Pictures; p.35 UPI/Bettmann; pp.39, 40 The Bettmann Archive; p.41 Culver Pictures; p.42 The Bettmann Archive; p.43 UPI/Bettmann; pp. 47, 48 The Cincinnati Zoo; p.49 Smithsonian Institution; pp.53, 54, 55 Courtesy Archives & Manuscripts, University Libraries, Arizona State University; p.59 The Bettmann Archive; p.61 Culver Pictures; p.62 © Murray & Associates/TSW; p.63 © Byron Crader/Ric Ergenbright Photography; p.67 Culver Pictures; p.68 The Bettmann Archive; pp.69,70 Culver Pictures; p.71 The Bettmann Archive; pp.75, 76 UPI/Bettmann; p.77 The Bettmann Archive; p.78 UPI/Bettmann; p. 79 (left) The Boston Athenæum; pp. 79 (right), 83 Culver Pictures; pp. 84, 85 UPI/Bettmann.

To teacher: This product is reflective of its time. When necessary to the content and understanding of the story, we have chosen to use the names by which ethnic groups were known at that time.

Headlines of the Century 1910-1919

In 1910 the world was at peace. This calm was shattered by World War I (1914-1918). The United States entered the war in 1917. World War I brought huge changes to Europe. Old nations disappeared while new ones were created. By the end of the war, the United States had the world's strongest military and economy. But America also had problems. For example, many people were poor. Also, African Americans often could not vote or live where they wanted.

Contents

THE FIGHT OF THE CENTURY

July 4, 1910—It's the Fight of the Century! Today Jack Johnson climbs into the ring to meet ex-champ Jim Jeffries. Boxing fans have waited over a year to see this fight. Johnson is the first black fighter to be heavyweight champ. Most black boxing fans hope he will win again. But white fans are pulling for Jim Jeffries. They are calling him The Great White Hope.

Jack Johnson climbs into the ring.

The New Champ

Before Jack Johnson, no African American had ever held the heavyweight boxing **title**. Every champion had been white. On December 26, 1908, heavyweight champ Tommy Burns fought African American Jack Johnson. The crowd cheered wildly for Burns. They met Johnson with boos.

Johnson paid no **attention** to the crowd. He simply went out and attacked Burns. In the 14th round, he knocked out Burns. Johnson had become the heavyweight champion of the world.

White boxing fans were angered. They wanted a white champ. Over the next few months, many white boxers tried to beat Johnson. They all failed. Then a **famous** writer named Jack London got an idea. "Jim Jeffries was a great white boxer," he said. "No one ever beat him. I bet he could beat Johnson easily."

The Great White Hope

It was true that Jim Jeffries had never lost a fight. He had been heavyweight champ for six years. But Jeffries had **retired** in 1905. He was now a farmer and weighed more than 300 pounds. Still, white fans like London pushed Jeffries to leave his farm. They begged him to fight Johnson.

Finally Jeffries agreed. For nearly a year he trained to get back in shape. He ran, skipped rope, and boxed. Slowly the extra pounds melted away. White boxing fans were excited. They felt sure they had found the right man to beat Johnson. Fans bet millions of dollars on Jeffries to win.

Johnson trained hard, too. But he found time to have fun, as well. Some people thought he wasn't taking the fight **seriously**. They were wrong. Jack Johnson was **determined** to hold on to his title.

Johnson trains for the fight.

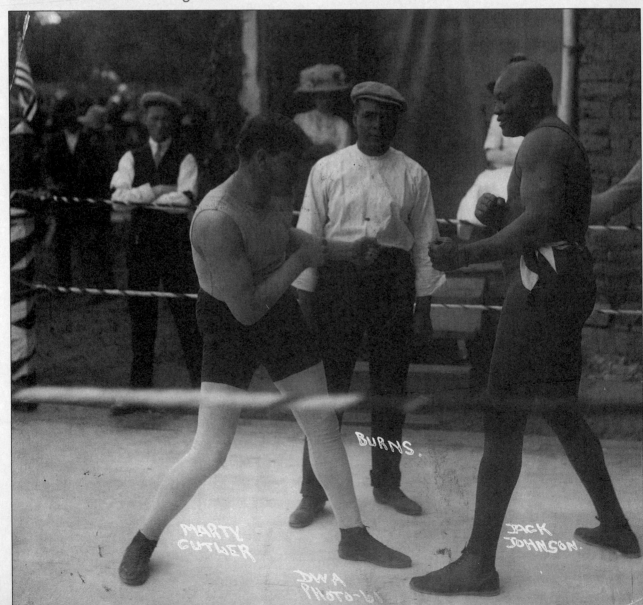

The Fight of the Century

No Contest

At last the big day arrived. More than 16,000 fans crowded around the boxing ring in Reno. In the first round, Jeffries came straight at Johnson. The champ just **glided** from side to side. Jeffries swung at Johnson, but many times he missed the mark.

In the third round, Johnson went on the attack. He hit Jeffries with a **powerful** left **jab**. There was a look of surprise on Jeffries' face. Johnson flashed his famous smile. "Come on now, Mr. Jeff," he said. "Let me see what you've got. Do something, man."

But there was nothing Jeffries could do. By the seventh round, people who knew boxing could see that Jeffries was a beaten man. The fight continued until the 15th round. Then Johnson knocked out Jeffries. "The Fight of the Century" was over. Jack Johnson had **proved** once again that he was the best boxer in the world.

Building Vocabulary

Part A

■ Write the best word to complete the sentence. Use each word once.

retired	title	powerful	proved

Jack Johnson was the first African American to hold the

heavyweight boxing (1)_____ . In 1910, a (2)_____

white boxer named Jim Jeffries tried to beat Johnson. Johnson was

more (3)_____ than Jeffries. When the two men fought,

Johnson (4)_____ that he was the best boxer in the world.

Part B

■ Match each word with its meaning.

____ 1. famous   a. moved smoothly

____ 2. glided   b. a quick punch

____ 3. jab   c. willing to try without giving up

____ 4. attention   d. without joking

____ 5. seriously   e. well known

____ 6. determined   f. watching or listening

Writing Your Ideas

■ If you could be the best in the world at something, what would it be?
On a separate sheet of paper explain why you chose what you did.

Remembering What You Read

■ Answer the questions.

1. Why were white boxing fans upset when Johnson became world champion?_____

_____

_____

2. How had Jeffries changed since he left boxing?_____

_____

_____

3. How did Jeffries get ready for his fight with Johnson?_____

_____

_____

4. How did the Fight of the Century end? _____

_____

_____

Thinking Critically—Main Ideas

■ Underline the two most important ideas from the story.

1. In 1910 white boxing fans wanted their champion to be white.

2. Jack London wanted to see Jim Jeffries fight Jack Johnson.

3. Jim Jeffries worked hard to get in shape for his 1910 fight.

4. Jack Johnson proved that he was the best boxer in 1910.

5. Boxing fans could tell that Jim Jeffries was losing the fight.

NEW STAR DISCOVERED

October 14, 1910—Williamina Fleming has discovered another new star! Mrs. Fleming has spent 29 years studying the night sky. During this time she has found amazing things. She has discovered more stars than any other person in the history of the world. Now Mrs. Fleming has added one more to her list. This special star suddenly becomes very bright, then fades out again.

A Talented Woman

"Mina" Fleming grew up in Scotland. She became a school teacher at the age of 14. In 1877, when she was 20 years old, she married James Fleming. The next year she and her husband moved to America.

The Flemings hoped for a good life in America. But trouble developed. After a few months in their new home, their marriage failed. Mina Fleming left her husband and headed out on her own. By then she was expecting a baby.

Alone, Mina had no money. She needed a job right away. Luckily she found work as a maid in the home of Dr. and Mrs. Edward Pickering.

Dr. Pickering was a young scientist. He was in charge of the telescope at Harvard College **Observatory**. The telescope was used to study the sky. It helped **astronomers** see the sun, moon, stars, and planets.

Williamina Fleming, a great astronomer

Dr. Pickering hired Mina to work in his observatory.

At first, Mina Fleming worked around the Pickering home. She did things maids usually do. She cleaned, sewed, and cooked. Soon, however, Dr. Pickering noticed that his maid was a special person. She was hard working, well **organized**, and smart.

"I could use someone like her around the observatory," Dr. Pickering told his wife. "We are behind in our work. Every night we take pictures of stars. The pictures have to be studied. The **position** of each star has to be written down. And somehow all the pictures need to be organized for later use. Mina is a good worker. Do you think she would like to work at the observatory?"

"I don't know," said Mrs. Pickering. "Why don't you ask her?"

Dr. Pickering did ask Mina. And Mina happily agreed. By the summer of 1879, she was spending part of each day at the Harvard College Observatory. At first, she did simple jobs. She added numbers and wrote down information.

Mina took pride in her work. She was careful not to make mistakes. She believed that every task should be done correctly.

Studying the Stars

In the fall of 1879, Mina had her baby. She named her son Edward Pickering Fleming. Dr. Pickering had opened up a whole new world for her. He had shown her the wonders of the night sky.

Soon after her baby was born, Mina went back to work as the Pickerings' maid. She also went back to work in the observatory.

As the months went by, Pickering developed great trust in Mina. He saw that she could do more than just add numbers. She helped with all sorts of difficult tasks. She could measure the **brightness** of stars. She could figure out their **exact** place in the sky. Dr. Pickering gave her harder and harder jobs. Mina performed all of them well.

By 1881 Mina Fleming was no longer a maid. She was a full-time worker at the observatory. In 1896 she took charge of all observatory photographs. She studied every star in every photograph.

The Draper Catalog

Mina studied the stars looking at photographs like this.

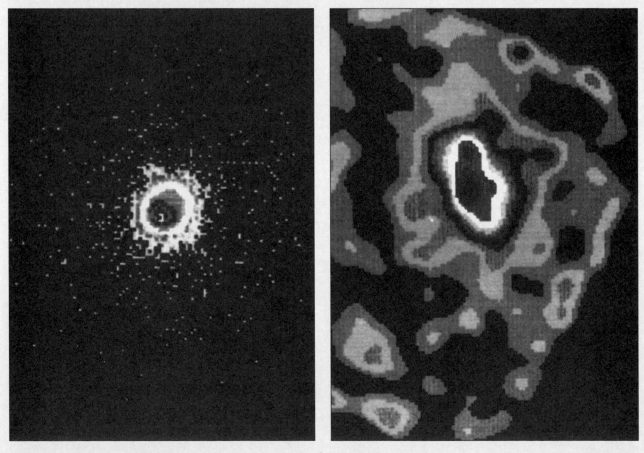

Today computers help astronomers study the stars.

She figured out what kind of star it was. Then she listed it in its correct **class**. She even helped Dr. Pickering come up with new classes when necessary. These new classes of stars became part of a famous **system**. It was called the Pickering-Fleming system.

As the years went by, Mina hired people to help her. She was careful to get good workers. Thinking of her own life, she made a point of hiring women. Soon she had 18 people—all women—working for her. Each of them did important work. But it was still Mina who knew the stars best. She could look at a photograph of hundreds of stars and see a new star in the group. She could also tell if an old star had changed in any way. Her knowledge of stars became greater than Dr. Pickering's own knowledge.

A Great Astronomer

By 1890 Mina Fleming had studied over 10,000 stars. She had recorded their color, brightness, and position in the sky. She published this information in a book. The book was called *The Draper Catalog of Stellar Spectra*. Her book became an important tool for astronomers at that time.

Mina Fleming did not stop there. For a long time, she had been interested in **variable** stars. These were stars that changed in brightness. Mina found that there were more of these stars than anyone imagined. She discovered 222 new ones. She spent a long time studying variable stars called **novas**. The brightness of a nova could change in a few short hours. Mina discovered ten new novas. She also discovered 94 hot, green-white stars called Wolf-Rayets.

By 1910 Mina Fleming was famous. People all over the world knew about her work with stars. She had done many things never done by astronomers before. She was the first woman to have an official job at Harvard University. She was an expert on "white dwarf" stars and on many other wonders of the night. Mina had also discovered more stars than any other person in history.

Sadly, by 1910 Mina was also sick. She found out she had stomach cancer. Bravely she continued her work with stars. Finally she died on May 21, 1922. The world had lost a great astronomer. Few who came after Mina Fleming have added as much as she had given us about the stars above.

Building Vocabulary

■ Use the clues to complete the puzzle. Choose from the words in the box.

variable
position
novas
astronomers
brightness
class
observatory
exact
system
organized

Across

1. where something is
5. people who study stars
8. likely to change
9. a way of doing something
10. how much light something gives

Down

2. building where stars are studied
3. kept in order
4. stars that suddenly become very bright
6. completely right
7. a group of things that are alike in some way

Writing Your Ideas

■ Why was Williamina Fleming successful? How did luck play a part? On a separate sheet of paper, write what you think.

Remembering What You Read

■ Some of the statements below are true. Others are false. Place a check in front of the three things that happened in the story.

_____ 1. Mina Fleming attended Harvard College.

_____ 2. At first, Mina Fleming worked as Dr. Pickering's maid.

_____ 3. Mina Fleming married Dr. Edward Pickering.

_____ 4. Mina Fleming recorded information on over 10,000 stars.

_____ 5. Mina Fleming discovered many new stars.

Building Skills—Use a Diagram

■ The diagram below shows the steps followed when studying stars. Look at the diagram, then answer the questions.

a. Take a photograph of stars.

b. Write down the position of each star.

c. Measure the brightness of each star.

d. List each star in its correct class.

e. Develop new classes of stars as needed.

1. What is the first step in studying the stars?_____

_____

2. Which is done first: finding the position of a star or measuring its brightness? _____

_____

3. One step is not always necessary. Which step is it?_____

_____

SPEEDWAY SPECTACULAR!

May 30, 1911—It was a big day for racing fans. At 6:30 this morning, the gates of the Indianapolis Speedway opened. Thousands of people poured in. They came to watch the first Indianapolis 500-Mile Race. The "Indy 500" was the longest auto race ever. Drivers raced their cars around the track at speeds of up to 100 miles per hour. Some cars broke down. Some crashed. But by the end of the day, one racer had won the $35,000 first-place prize.

Indy 500 founders pose with Henry Ford—Henry Ford, Arthur Newby, Frank Wheeler, Carl Fisher, James Allison.

One Man's Dream

The Indy 500 was the dream of a man named Carl G. Fisher. Fisher lived in Indianapolis. He wanted his city to be the auto center of America. "A huge race track would help make that happen," he thought. And so in 1909, Fisher built the Indianapolis Speedway. It was a two and one half mile **oval** track. The surface was a mixture of crushed **limestone** and **gravel**. This was fine for very short races. But it was a **disaster** for long races.

Fisher discovered this when he tried to hold a 300-mile race at the new track. As the cars circled the speedway, their tires kicked up dirt. Soon huge clouds of dust hung in the air. The 16 racers **struggled** to see through the blinding **haze**. After less than 200 miles, two drivers spun off into the stands. Three people were killed. Several others were badly hurt. Fisher felt terrible. He stopped the race before anyone else got hurt.

A Brick Track

"I guess this means no more long races . . ." Fisher thought sadly. But then he had an idea. What if he removed the dirt?

What if he **paved** the whole track with bricks?

This was not easy to do. Workers spent many months laying ten-pound bricks over the track. They used more than three million bricks in all. At last, the paving was finished. Fisher planned to open the brick track by holding a big race. He set it for Memorial Day, 1911. "It will be the biggest sports event ever!" he cried. "Forty of the world's best auto racers in a 500-mile contest! There's never been anything like it before."

Fisher was right. The Indianapolis 500-Mile Race was **spectacular**. Fisher had hoped 40,000 fans might come. On race day 80,000 fans showed up. Excitement hung in the air. Who would win the huge first-place prize?

Most of the race cars carried two people. One person drove. The other was the mechanic. The mechanic kept watch for cars coming up from behind. One car, however, held only one man. Ray Harroun did not want a mechanic. He wanted to race alone. The other drivers didn't like his idea.

The first Indy 500

Ray Harroun—winner of the first Indy 500

"He won't know when we're passing him!" they cried. "That's dangerous for all of us." Harroun answered them by fitting a mirror on the front of his car. It was the world's first rear-view mirror.

The Winner!

When the race began, the drivers took off. After just 12 of the 200 **laps**, driver Art Greiner lost control. His car **slammed** into a wall. Mechanic Sam Dickson was killed. Later in the race, a mechanic fell out of a car. This caused a huge crash. Other problems came up. Engine oil spilled onto the track, making cars skid and slide. Near the end of the race, drivers were just trying to hang on. Finally, after 6 hours and 42 minutes, a car crossed the finish line. Ray Harroun, the single driver, had won the race!

Building Vocabulary

■ Read each sentence. Fill in the circle next to the best meaning for the word in dark print. You may use the glossary.

1. Fisher built an **oval** track.
   ○ a. egg-shaped   ○ b. very large   ○ c. dirt

2. The track was made using **limestone**.
   ○ a. green grass   ○ b. wood   ○ c. a kind of rock

3. **Gravel** was put on the track.
   ○ a. paint   ○ b. bits of rock   ○ c. big signs

4. The first long race was a **disaster**.
   ○ a. terrible happening   ○ b. great success   ○ c. secret

5. The racers **struggled** to see through the dust.
   ○ a. did not try   ○ b. raced each other   ○ c. worked hard

6. The **haze** made the race dangerous.
   ○ a. dust in the air   ○ b. driving rain   ○ c. strong winds

7. Fisher **paved** the track with bricks.
   ○ a. paid for   ○ b. made bigger   ○ c. covered

8. The race was **spectacular**.
   ○ a. not well known   ○ b. boring   ○ c. wonderful

9. The racers had to go 500 **laps**.
   ○ a. miles   ○ b. trips around the track   ○ c. minutes

10. His car **slammed** into a wall.
    ○ a. flew over   ○ b. hit hard   ○ c. just missed

Writing Your Ideas

■ Imagine you are watching the first Indy 500. On a separate sheet of paper, write what you think of the race.

Remembering What You Read

■ Answer the questions.

1. Why did Fisher build the track in Indianapolis? _____
_____

2. Why did Fisher decide to cover the track with bricks?_____
_____

3. Why did Ray Harroun put a mirror on front of his car?_____
_____
_____

4. What difficulties did the first Indy 500 racers face?_____
_____
_____
_____

Thinking Critically—Fact or Opinion

■ Write **F** before each fact. Write **O** before each opinion.

_____ 1. Car racing is the most exciting sport in the world.

_____ 2. Most of the race cars held two people in the first Indy 500.

_____ 3. Long races are more fun than short ones.

_____ 4. The Indianapolis Speedway is two and a half miles long.

_____ 5. The first Indianapolis 500 was held on Memorial Day.

_____ 6. Ray Harroun was braver than the other drivers.

_____ 7. Engine oil spilled onto the track during the race.

_____ 8. Mechanics should not ride with the drivers.

MONA LISA STOLEN!

August 22, 1911—The art world is in shock! Police have just announced that the world-famous painting *Mona Lisa* has been stolen. The painting had been hanging in the Louvre, a museum in Paris, France. Yesterday, however, guards discovered it missing. Sixty police detectives are working on the case. So far, there are no answers. There is only fear that the most beautiful painting ever made is lost forever.

The *Mona Lisa*

The Mysterious Smile of *Mona Lisa*

The *Mona Lisa* was painted in the early 1500s. The artist was an Italian man named Leonardo da Vinci. Leonardo had created many great **works**. But the painting called the *Mona Lisa* is one of his most famous works. People say there is something almost magical about the painting. The painting shows a woman, Lisa del Gioconda, smiling **mysteriously**. The smile makes her look both happy and sad at the same time.

Over the years millions of people have **admired** this smile. They have come from around the world to view the *Mona Lisa*.

Leonardo painted the *Mona Lisa* in Italy. But by 1911 it was hanging in the Louvre Museum in France. The Louvre had many guards to protect the museum's **treasures**. But the guards did not save the *Mona Lisa*.

Until it was stolen, no one worried about the *Mona Lisa*. People thought it was too famous to be stolen. No thief could ever sell it. Everyone

The Louvre

would **recognize** it. Everyone would know it was stolen property.

On August 21, 1911, however, the *Mona Lisa* was stolen. It happened on a cleaning day, when the Louvre was closed to visitors. Only workers were supposed to be in the museum. About seven o'clock in the morning, some new workers walked past the *Mona Lisa* with their boss.

"They say this painting is worth more than any other in the Louvre," the boss said. "Take a good look at it. On some days guards take it upstairs to a private room. When they do, **photographers** can take pictures of it."

An hour later, the workers passed the spot again. The *Mona Lisa* was gone! Four empty hooks were left hanging from the wall.

"The guards must have taken it upstairs," the boss said.

Missing!

The next day the Louvre was open to visitors. Many noticed that the *Mona Lisa* was missing.

But everyone thought it was with photographers. At noon, one guard decided to check. He was **horrified** to learn that the painting was not upstairs.

Quickly the guards called the police. On a back stairway, police found the *Mona Lisa*'s frame. The painting itself was not there. Police questioned all museum workers. No one knew what had happened. By the end of the day, the truth was clear. The *Mona Lisa* had been stolen.

The world was shocked. This feeling soon turned to anger. Many people blamed the museum.

Why wasn't the *Mona Lisa* better protected? Why weren't guards watching the painting at all times? The people in charge of the Louvre could not explain.

Police tried to piece together the **crime**. They spoke with the guard posted near the *Mona Lisa* that morning. He had left his station to take a break. This meant the thief had plenty of time to walk up to the painting, pull it off its hooks, and walk away.

Who would have done such a thing? Many thought the thief must be crazy. Maybe he or she had fallen in love with the *Mona Lisa*.

Leonardo's self-portrait

Tête	longr	1.7	Pied g.	25.3	Coulr de l'iris g.	n° de cl.	5-4	Cheveux	ch
	largr	15.1	Médius g.	11.0		aurle c mar cl		Barbe	ch
	zygrs	13.3	Auricre g.	8.5		péri ant bf		Teint Pon	m
	Oreille dr.	6.6	Coudée g.	43.1		partés		Main dr.	
								Main g.	

Peruggia 25.1.09   378.699

Vincenzo as photographed by police

Guards remembered one visitor who often sat for hours, admiring the painting. The museum had received many letters addressed to *Mona Lisa*. Perhaps one of the writers was the thief. Police followed these **clues**, but the clues led nowhere.

A Surprise Ending

As the months passed, most people gave up hope. Everyone thought the *Mona Lisa* was gone forever. Louvre directors hung a different painting in its place. Then,

two years after the crime, a strange letter arrived in Florence, Italy. It was addressed to an art dealer named Alfredo Geri. The letter was written by a man calling himself Leonardo Vincenzo. In the letter Vincenzo **claimed** to have the *Mona Lisa*. He said he wanted to sell it to someone in Italy. He wanted the painting to be back in its true home.

At first, Geri thought the letter was a joke. But he answered it, anyway. He said he would gladly buy the real *Mona Lisa*.

28

But to be sure it was real, Geri said he would have to look at it. One day Vincenzo showed up in Geri's shop. He said he had the *Mona Lisa* in a nearby hotel.

Geri grew excited. Maybe this man really had the *Mona Lisa*. Geri told the police. The next day, December 11, 1913, he went to Vincenzo's hotel room. Geri watched in wonder as Vincenzo opened an old trunk and took out the *Mona Lisa*.

Geri checked the painting to be sure it was real. He looked to see if it had been harmed. He then called the police to get Vincenzo.

They found out that Vincenzo was really an Italian named Vincenzo Peruggia. He had once been a workman at the Louvre. There he had seen the *Mona Lisa*. He knew it had been painted by an Italian. He wanted the painting returned to Italy. So on August 21, 1911, he had put on his work clothes. He had slipped into the Louvre and walked off with the painting. It was as simple as that.

Alfredo Geri collected a reward for his part in returning the painting. Vincenzo Peruggia was sent to jail. And the *Mona Lisa* was sent back to the Louvre, where it still hangs today.

The *Mona Lisa* hangs in the Louvre today.

Building Vocabulary

■ To complete the sentences choose a word from the box. Write the word on the blanks after the sentence. The letters in the boxes will spell the answer to question 10.

recognize	crime	admired	mysteriously	works
horrified	clues	claimed	photographers	

1. Guards thought the painting was with _____. __ __ __ ☐ __ __ __ __ __ __ __

2. Da Vinci's works are much _____. __ __ __ __ ☐ __ __

3. Can you _____ the *Mona Lisa*? __ ☐ __ __ __ __ __ __ __

4. Vincenzo _____ to have the real *Mona Lisa*. __ __ ☐ __ __ __ __

5. Da Vinci created many great _____. __ __ __ __ ☐

6. The police looked for _____. __ __ ☐ __ __ __

7. Guards were _____ to learn that the painting was gone. __ __ ☐ __ __ __ __ __ __

8. Stealing is a _____. __ __ __ __ ☐

9. *Mona Lisa* smiles _____. __ __ ☐ __ __ __ __ __ __ __ __

10. What is kept in the Louvre Museum? _____

Writing Your Ideas

■ Imagine you work at the Louvre. On a separate sheet of paper, write a paragraph that explains why you think the *Mona Lisa* is smiling so mysteriously.

Remembering What You Read

■ Fill in the circle next to the best ending for each sentence.

1. At first, guards thought the *Mona Lisa* was with
   ○ a. police.   ○ b. photographers.   ○ c. Alfredo Geri.

2. Police had no luck finding the
   ○ a. stolen painting.   ○ b. Louvre Museum.
   ○ c. missing guard.

3. Vincenzo showed Geri
   ○ a. a photograph.   ○ b. a police report.   ○ c. the *Mona Lisa*.

4. Vincenzo stole the *Mona Lisa* because he wanted it
   ○ a. for himself.   ○ b. in Italy.   ○ c. in France.

Building Skills—Read a Table

■ Use the table below to answer the questions.

Famous Paintings by Italian Artists			
Name of Work	Artist	Subject	Years Painted
Mona Lisa	Da Vinci		1503-1508
Sistine Chapel	Michelangelo	Bible stories	1508-1511
School of Athens	Raphael	Greek teachers	1510-1511

1. What was the subject of the *Mona Lisa*? Write your answer in the correct place in the table.

2. When was the work *School of Athens* painted? _____

3. Who painted the *Sistine Chapel*? _____

JIM THORPE CAPTURES GOLD!

July 15, 1912—As the crowd roared wildly, King Gustav told Jim Thorpe what everyone was thinking. "Sir," he said, "you are the greatest athlete in the world." The Olympic Games ended today in Stockholm, Sweden. The crowd greeted all athletes warmly as they accepted their medals. But people saved their biggest cheer for Jim Thorpe, winner of two gold medals.

Mayor of New York City shakes hands with Thorpe in a parade for Olympic winners.

A Born Athlete

Jim Thorpe was born on May 28, 1888, in what is now Oklahoma. His mother came from the Potawatomie and Kickapoo peoples. His father was part Sac and Fox. Thorpe's **tribal** name was Wa-Tho-Huck, or "Bright Path."

The young boy grew up on a farm. He learned to ride a horse and swim when he was only three. Sadly, Thorpe's mother died when he was just 12 years old. His father died three years later. In 1904, Thorpe entered Carlisle, a small government-run school in Pennsylvania.

At first, no one at Carlisle knew Thorpe was a great athlete. Even Thorpe did not know it. Then one day he saw boys on the track team trying to do the high jump. They could not clear the bar. "I can do better than that," Thorpe thought. On an **impulse**, he ran across the field. Even in boots and heavy street clothes, he jumped easily over the bar. The coach believed Thorpe had great **potential** as an athlete.

33

Soon after that, Thorpe joined the school football team. In his first game he ran for 150 yards and scored two **touchdowns**. By the end of the football season, Thorpe was the "most talked-about athlete" in the state. Soon the whole country had heard of Thorpe. Twice he was named an All-American football player. He also became a star in track, baseball, and tennis.

On to the Olympics

In 1912 Jim Thorpe joined the U.S. Olympic team. He entered two **events**—the pentathlon and decathlon. The pentathlon is five track and field contests. The decathlon is ten. In the pentathlon, Thorpe won four of the five contests. He got a gold medal.

Next came the decathlon. This was Thorpe's first decathlon. Still, he earned more points than anyone ever had before. Thorpe won another gold medal. He became the first person ever to win both events. When he received his medals on July 15, 1912, he truly was the greatest athlete in the world.

Thorpe throws the javelin.

Thorpe poses for photo at Stockholm Olympics.

A Hard Blow

In January 1913 trouble **arose**. The U.S. Olympic **Committee** learned Thorpe had once earned $25 a week playing baseball. Getting paid for a sport was against Olympic rules.

Thorpe tried to explain that he had made an **honest** mistake. He told the committee, "I did not know that I was doing wrong. I was just doing what other **college** men had done . . ."

The Olympic Committee refused to listen. Thorpe was ordered to give back his medals. His name was crossed out of the Olympic record book. Losing his medals **shattered** Thorpe's world. Thorpe thought about the gold medals that had been taken away until he died in 1953.

In 1982 the Olympic Committee thought over Thorpe's trouble again. They put his name back into the record book. They gave Thorpe's medals to his children. Jim Thorpe, one of the greatest athletes of all time, was again an Olympic champion.

Building Vocabulary

■ To complete the sentences choose a word from the box. Write the word on the blanks after the sentence. The letters in the boxes will spell the answer to question 10.

touchdowns	arose	honest	impulse	potential
committee	events	tribal	college	

1. Thorpe had an _____ to jump over the bar.   _ _ _ _ _ □ _

2. Thorpe made an _____ mistake.   □ _ _ _ _ _

3. In January 1913 trouble _____.   □ _ _ _ _

4. Thorpe won gold medals in two _____.   _ _ _ _ □ _

5. Thorpe's coach saw that he had great _____.   _ _ _ _ _ □ _ _ _

6. The _____ took Thorpe's medals.   _ _ _ _ _ _ _ □ _

7. Thorpe's _____ name was Wa-Tho-Huck.   _ □ _ _ _ _

8. Thorpe did not go to _____.   _ _ _ _ □ _ _

9. In football Thorpe scored many _____.   _ _ _ _ _ □ _ _ _

10. Thorpe's world was_____.

Writing Your Ideas

■ Imagine you are Jim Thorpe. On a separate sheet of paper, write a letter to a good friend. Describe how you feel when your gold medals are taken away.

Remembering What You Read

■ Fill in the circle next to the best ending for each sentence.

1. At Carlisle, Jim Thorpe became
   ○ a. sick.   ○ b. a Kickapoo leader.   ○ c. a sports star.

2. Jim Thorpe won two Olympic gold medals in
   ○ a. track and field.   ○ b. football.   ○ c. boxing.

3. Thorpe lost his medals because he had earned money
   ○ a. as a teacher.   ○ b. playing baseball.   ○ c. writing books.

4. After Thorpe died, the Olympic Committee
   ○ a. became angry.   ○ b. changed their decision.
   ○ c. broke up.

Thinking Critically—Conclusions

■ Finish each sentence by writing the best answer.

1. Jim Thorpe went to Carlisle because_____

   _____

   _____

2. Jim Thorpe lost his medals because_____

   _____

   _____

3. Thorpe felt terrible because_____

   _____

   _____

4. Jim Thorpe's children were given his medals because_____

   _____

ARCHDUKE FERDINAND SHOT

June 28, 1914—Today in Sarajevo, Bosnia, a young man rushed forward and fired several shots. Archduke Francis Ferdinand and his wife have been killed! The killer then tried to shoot himself. However, someone in the crowd knocked the gun from his hand. European leaders fear the murders will lead to bigger trouble in this part of the world.

Danger in Bosnia

In 1914 Francis Ferdinand was next in line to be **emperor** of Austria. That made him important. It also put him in danger. Anyone who wanted to hurt Austria might try to hurt Ferdinand.

The biggest danger came from the Serbs. Serbia was a small, weak neighbor of Austria. But Serbs didn't live only in Serbia. Many Serbs lived in lands controlled by Austria. One of these lands was Bosnia.

Serbs in Bosnia didn't like being part of Austria. They wanted Bosnia to break away. They wanted Bosnia to become part of Serbia. They wanted Serbia to become a larger, stronger country. Many Serbs in Bosnia thought Austria was the enemy. Ferdinand knew this. Yet, in 1914, he decided to visit Bosnia anyway.

"Don't go!" his friends begged him. "It's too dangerous." But Ferdinand would not change his mind. He had two reasons for making the trip. First, he thought he might do some good. He might be able to **calm** the Serbs.

Archduke Ferdinand and Sophie in Sarajevo

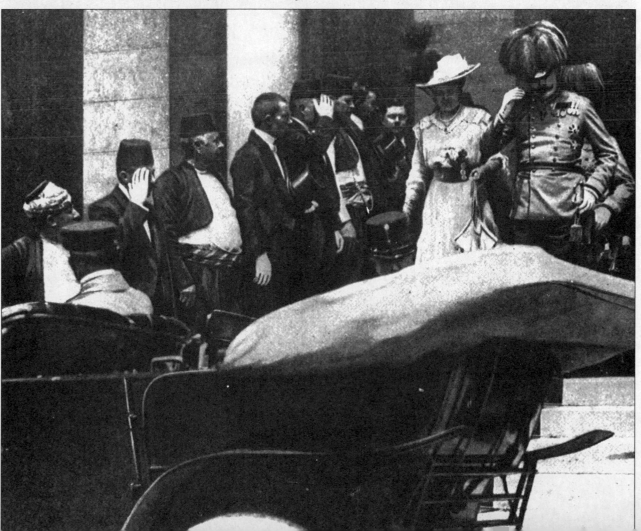

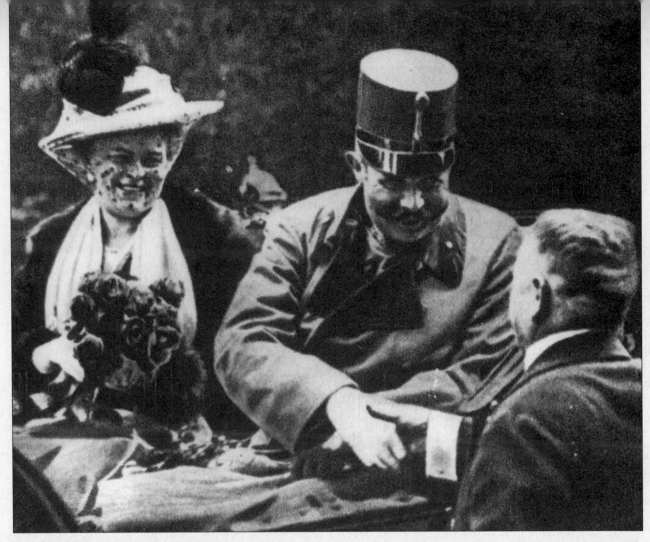
Archduke Ferdinand and Sophie an hour before they are shot

Second, Ferdinand wanted to honor his wife. Sophie was not loved by Austrians. She did not come from a rich or important family. Many Austrians did not think she deserved to be part of the **royal** family. A law had been passed so that none of her children could ever become emperor. Sophie was not even allowed to ride in the royal coach with her husband.

"We have been married 14 years now," thought Ferdinand. "Yet Sophie still does not get the honor she deserves. If we visit Bosnia, things will be different. We will be Austrian visitors. The Bosnians will have to be nice to her. It will be my special present to her."

The Murder Plan

But murder plans were taking shape in Sarajevo, Bosnia. Seven young Serbians wanted to strike a blow for freedom. They thought killing the Archduke would do this. On the morning of June 28, 1914, these students chose places along important streets of the city. They waited for the Archduke to ride by on his way to City Hall.

Each of the students carried a gun or a **bomb**. They also carried poison. The one who killed the Archduke would quickly swallow the poison. That way the police would not be able to make any **arrests**.

There were four cars in the royal parade. The Archduke and Sophie were riding in the second car. As the cars crossed a bridge, they passed the first Serbian student. He held his bomb tightly in his hand. But at the last moment, he lost his **courage**. He let the cars pass slowly by.

Just down the street stood the second young Serb. His name was Nedjelko Cabrinovic. Cabrinovic did not lose his nerve. He took careful aim and tossed his bomb right at Ferdinand's head.

At that moment, the car gained speed. The bomb just missed Sophie. Ferdinand saw the bomb fly through the air. He raised his arm to protect his wife.

Drawing of the attack

The bomb hit his arm and fell to the street before it **exploded**. The blast hurt three people in the third car. It also **injured** several people standing along the street. Cabrinovic quickly swallowed his poison. But the poison was too weak to kill him. It only made him sick. The police captured him easily.

After the attack the driver of Ferdinand's car drove much faster. The car sped past three more of the Serbian students. These Serbs had no time to attack. Finally, Ferdinand reached City Hall. There he screamed to the mayor, "Mr. Mayor, this is **outrageous**! We come to Sarajevo on a visit and a bomb is thrown at us!"

After a few minutes, Ferdinand calmed down. He gave a friendly speech to the crowd outside City Hall. Then he decided to visit the hospital. He wanted to check on the people hurt by the bomb.

The Spark of War

The parade of cars started off again. As they crossed another bridge, they passed the sixth student. Like the first student, he lost his nerve and did nothing.

Newspapers around the world report the attack.

42

Minutes later, the car passed the last of the young Serbs. Nineteen-year-old Gavrilo Princip pulled out his gun and fired. One shot hit the Archduke in the neck. Another hit Sophie in the stomach. Within minutes both she and Ferdinand were dead.

To some the murder of Ferdinand and Sophie was just a sad story. But to others it was the beginning of big trouble. Austrian leaders blamed Serbia for the two murders. Serbia did not want a war. But Austrian leaders kept pushing. On July 28, Austria **declared** war against Serbia.

Other nations in Europe watched this war start and took sides. Germany, Hungary, and Turkey sided with Austria. Russia, France, and Great Britain joined with Serbia. By August 1, 1914, a huge war had begun. These events were the start of World War I. The murder of two people would lead to the death of ten million others.

Gavrilo Princip is arrested.

Building Vocabulary

■ Match each word with its meaning.

____ 1. courage a. become quieter

____ 2. emperor b. being held in jail

____ 3. arrests c. having to do with a king or queen

____ 4. exploded d. shocking and hard to believe

____ 5. calm e. being brave

____ 6. outrageous f. burst apart

____ 7. royal g. ruler of a group of countries

Part B

■ Write the best word to complete each sentence. Use each word once.

injured	declared	bomb

When Archduke Ferdinand visited Bosnia, a Serbian student

threw a (1)_____ at him. Ferdinand was not (2)_____.

Later that day, however, he was shot and killed by another Serb. A

month later, Austria (3)_____ war on Serbia.

Writing Your Ideas

■ On a separate sheet of paper, write three important facts you learned from this story.

Remembering What You Read

■ Some of the statements below are true. Others are false. Place a check in front of the three things that happened in the story.

_____ 1. Ferdinand planned to kill his wife.

_____ 2. Serbian students planned to kill Ferdinand.

_____ 3. Sophie and Ferdinand visited Bosnia.

_____ 4. Ferdinand ran away to Hungary.

_____ 5. The mayor of Bosnia threw a bomb.

_____ 6. The killing of Archduke Ferdinand led to World War I.

Building Skills—Read a Graph

■ Use the following graph to answer the questions.

1. How many Americans were killed in battle in World War I?_____

_____

2. How many Americans were wounded but did not die?_____

_____

3. Did more Americans die in battle or in other ways?_____

_____

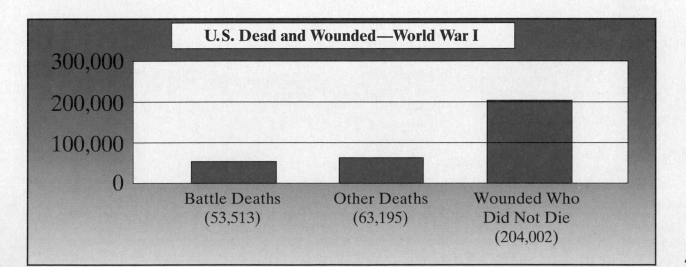

U.S. Dead and Wounded—World War I

Battle Deaths (53,513)	Other Deaths (63,195)	Wounded Who Did Not Die (204,002)

LAST PASSENGER PIGEON DIES

September 1, 1914—Never again will a passenger pigeon fly across the sky. Never again will its cry echo through the air. Martha the passenger pigeon is dead. The 29-year-old bird died today at a zoo in Cincinnati, Ohio. Martha's death is important and serious. Martha was the last passenger pigeon in the world. With her death the world has lost all birds of her kind. The passenger pigeon is now a thing of the past.

Martha, the last passenger pigeon

Billions of Birds

In the early 1800s, there were billions of passenger pigeons in North America. These birds traveled in huge **flocks**. When they passed by, they darkened the sky for hours. Looking up, all that could be seen was a huge cloud of flapping wings.

Passenger pigeons flew freely across the **continent**. This **species** of birds spent summers in the north. When winter came, they flew south. This earned the birds their name. Some people called them passengers because they passed from place to place.

Native American peoples knew all about passenger pigeons. The Chippewa, Mohawks, and Senecas hunted the birds. So did many other Native Americans. These people killed only what they could eat. Plenty of passenger pigeons were not harmed. Native Americans did not kill the birds at times when young birds needed to be fed.

Early white **settlers** followed the same pattern. Many needed the birds to feed their families. But they never killed more than they could eat.

Changes

By 1869, trains ran across the country. Food could be shipped long distances. Passenger pigeons could be sold as food. Hunters began shooting the birds in great numbers. The pigeons were shipped to the cities by train.

The birds soon became **endangered**. Hunters were killing thousands of passenger pigeons each day. The hunters did not **bother** to find all the birds they shot down. They just scooped up the bodies that were handy.

Passenger pigeon memorial at the Cincinnati Zoo

48

EXTINCT

You can see Martha at the Smithsonian in Washington D.C.

Sometimes half the dead birds were left to **rot**.

Too Late

To make things worse, people began killing passenger pigeons for **sport**. Some people **practiced** their aim by shooting the birds. Men held contests to see who could kill the most birds in one day. Every contest meant more passenger pigeons died.

Few passenger pigeons **survived**. By 1880 people saw their mistake and tried to do something about it. But it was too late. Some passenger pigeons were put in zoos to keep them safe. But by 1914 only Martha was left. When she died, the beautiful birds that had once passed so freely overhead passed into history forever.

49

Building Vocabulary

■ Read each sentence. Fill in the circle next to the best meaning for the word in dark print. You may use the glossary.

1. Many **flocks** of passenger pigeons could be seen.
   ○ a. cages   ○ b. groups   ○ c. pictures

2. The birds flew across the **continent**.
   ○ a. huge land area   ○ b. deep water   ○ c. mountains

3. One **species** of whales died out.
   ○ a. trainers   ○ b. certain group of animals   ○ c. color

4. **Settlers** shot birds for food.
   ○ a. people who move to new lands   ○ b. store owners
   ○ c. people who have many children

5. The birds **survived** for a while.
   ○ a. stayed hidden   ○ b. stayed alive   ○ c. stayed sick

6. Passenger pigeons became **endangered**.
   ○ a. close to dying out   ○ b. dangerous   ○ c. very healthy

7. Hunters did not **bother** to find all the birds they shot.
   ○ a. follow the law   ○ b. forget   ○ c. take the time

8. Many dead birds were left to **rot**.
   ○ a. disappear   ○ b. spoil   ○ c. scare other birds away

9. People killed passenger pigeons for **sport**.
   ○ a. fun   ○ b. money   ○ c. to stay alive

10. Hunters **practiced** their aim by shooting birds.
    ○ a. hurt   ○ b. grew big   ○ c. to do over and over

Writing Your Ideas

■ Imagine you are the zookeeper at the Cincinnati Zoo. On a separate sheet of paper, describe how you feel when Martha dies.

Remembering What You Read

■ Answer the questions.

1. How did passenger pigeons get their name?_____

_____

2. What was special about how Native Americans hunted passenger
pigeons?_____

_____

_____

3. What were two of the reasons why passenger pigeons died out?

_____

_____

4. Who was Martha?_____

_____

Thinking Critically—Main Ideas

■ Underline the two most important ideas from the story.

1. Native Americans hunted passenger pigeons for food.

2. By 1869 trains ran across the United States.

3. There used to be billions of passenger pigeons in America.

4. Passenger pigeons traveled in flocks.

5. People killed so many passenger pigeons that the species was
wiped out.

LET MY PEOPLE GO!

September 30, 1915—"Little by little the Indian's land is fading away. We must act as one. Our bodies and souls must be used to gain our freedom. I ask this of the United States—Let My People Go!"

These were the words of Carlos Montezuma. He spoke them today in Lawrence, Kansas. The Society of American Indians heard his words. Montezuma challenged the members to take bold action to improve their lives.

Early Life

Carlos Montezuma was born about 1867. He was a Yavapai Indian. His mother and father named him Wassaja. In 1871 Pima Indians attacked the Yavapais. They captured four-year-old Wassaja. The Pima sold him to a white man named Carlos Gentile. Young Wassaja never saw his family again. He later said, "I had been just a small boy in the wilds of Arizona, just as happy as a bird, free from any thought of danger." Wassaja didn't return to his Arizona homeland for nearly thirty years.

Gentile changed Wassaja's name. He called the child Carlos, after himself. He gave him the last name of Montezuma. Gentile was kind to Montezuma. He wanted him to have an **education**. So Gentile **enrolled** Montezuma in school.

Carlos Montezuma as a young man

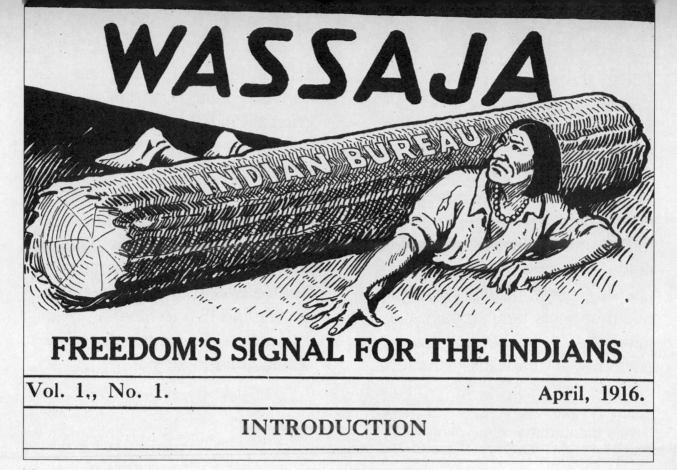

WASSAJA

FREEDOM'S SIGNAL FOR THE INDIANS

Vol. 1., No. 1.   April, 1916.

INTRODUCTION

Montezuma started a newspaper for Native Americans.

At first, Montezuma found school difficult. He didn't know how to read or write. But in time, Montezuma got used to his new life. He caught up to his classmates at school. He later told how he did it. "I stayed home at night to study while the other children played. Soon I learned as fast as any of the whites."

Life on the Reservation

Montezuma's hard work paid off. He went to college at a time when few people did so. In 1883 he **graduated** from college. Six years later he completed medical school.

He was one of the first Native Americans to become a doctor.

Montezuma then took a job with the U.S. **Bureau of Indian Affairs**. He thought this would be a good way to help his people. For several years Montezuma served as a Bureau of Indian Affairs doctor in North Dakota, Nevada, and Washington. It was a hard time for him. He liked working with his people. But he saw many things that made him angry. Montezuma did not like **reservations**. He felt that Native Americans were cut off from the rest of the country. He felt that the people in charge treated the Yavapai and other tribes unfairly.

Fighting for His People

In 1897 Montezuma quit the Bureau of Indian Affairs. He returned to Chicago to practice medicine there. But Montezuma continued to be **concerned** about Native Americans. He gave speeches. He spoke of the time in which they were living as being a time of change. Montezuma's ideas even led him to speak to the Society of American Indians in 1915. He wrote **articles** that were published in newspapers. He also started a monthly newspaper called *Wassaja*. Montezuma used the newspaper to speak out for better **treatment** of Native Americans. In the last issue of *Wassaja*, he wrote ". . . let us not be dismayed, let us not be **discouraged**, let us look up and go ahead and fight on for freedom and **citizenship** for our people."

Montezuma and his wife Mary in 1920

Building Vocabulary

■ Read each sentence. Fill in the circle next to the best meaning for the word in dark print. You may use the glossary.

1. Gentile made sure Montezuma got an **education**.
   ○ a. help from doctors   ○ b. lessons in school   ○ c. pet

2. Gentile **enrolled** Montezuma in school.
   ○ a. lost   ○ b. signed up for   ○ c. forgot about

3. Montezuma **graduated** from college in 1883.
   ○ a. disappeared   ○ b. finished   ○ c. became angry

4. Montezuma told his people not to be **discouraged**.
   ○ a. lose hope   ○ b. starting fights   ○ c. afraid

■ Match each word or group of words with its meaning.

____ 1. articles   a. the way people act towards others

____ 2. reservations   b. worried about

____ 3. Bureau of   c. land set aside for Native
        Indian Affairs   Americans

____ 4. treatment   d. reports written for newspapers

____ 5. citizenship   e. being a member of a country

____ 6. concerned   f. office set up to help
                                   Native Americans

Writing Your Ideas

■ Imagine you are Carlos Montezuma. On a separate sheet of paper, describe how you feel when you return to Arizona after being away for almost 30 years.

Remembering What You Read

■ Some of the statements below are true. Others are false. Place a check in front of the three things that happened in the story.

_____ 1. Carlos Gentile was sold to Wassaja.

_____ 2. Wassaja was given the name Carlos Montezuma.

_____ 3. Carlos Montezuma became a doctor.

_____ 4. Montezuma started a monthly newspaper.

_____ 5. Montezuma decided not to help Native Americans.

Building Skills—Use a Time Line

■ Use the time line to answer the questions.

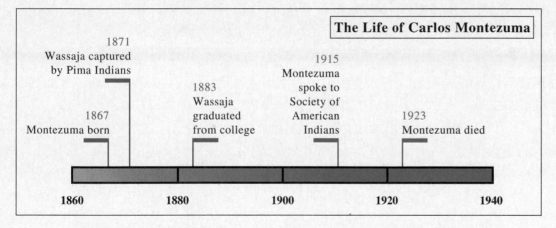

The Life of Carlos Montezuma

1867 Montezuma born
1871 Wassaja captured by Pima Indians
1883 Wassaja graduated from college
1915 Montezuma spoke to Society of American Indians
1923 Montezuma died

1860   1880   1900   1920   1940

1. What happened to Carlos Montezuma in 1871?_____

_____

2. What group did Montezuma speak to in 1915?_____

_____

3. When did Montezuma graduate from college?_____

4. What year did Montezuma die?_____

5. Add a mark and label the time line to show when Montezuma quit the Bureau of Indian Affairs.

MATA HARI ARRESTED!

February 13, 1917—French police have arrested the famous dancer Mata Hari. She has been charged with spying for the Germans. French police believe Mata Hari told the Germans about a new weapon called the tank. A few days ago, Mata Hari left Spain and came to Paris, France. Police say she came here to be paid for her spy work. If the French court finds Mata Hari guilty of spying for Germany, she may be shot to death.

Mata Hari, dancer and spy

Escape from Home

Mata Hari's real name was Margaretha Zelle. She was born in Leeuwarden, Holland, on August 7, 1876. Her father spent almost all his free time with his sons. He paid no attention to young Margaretha. Antie Zelle wasn't very close to her daughter, either. She couldn't understand why Margaretha spent so much time lost in dreams.

Margaretha had a **restless** mind. She wanted to meet new people and see new things. At the age of 18, she saw her chance to get away from home. She met and quickly married a Dutch army officer named Captain Rudolph MacLeod. He was more than twice her age.

MacLeod took Margaretha to the Dutch West Indies (now Indonesia). They lived there for a few years. MacLeod turned out to be a **violent** man, and Margaretha left him. But her time in the Dutch West Indies wasn't wasted. She spent many hours watching the island dancers. "I wonder," she thought, "if I could dance like that."

New Names, New Games

In 1902 Margaretha returned to Holland. There she continued to study dancing. Margaretha tried to find work as a dancer under her own name. But she had little luck. Then, in 1905, she had a great idea. "Why not change my name?" she thought. "With my black hair, dark eyes, and dark skin, I bet I could **pass** as a real Asian dancer."

Margaretha chose Mata Hari as her new name. It means "Eye of the Morning." She made up a new life story to go with her new name. She said, "I was born in the south of India. My mother was a **temple** dancer who died the day I was born. I danced for the first time in an Indian temple at the age of 13."

The plan worked perfectly. Margaretha, now using the name Mata Hari, fooled everyone. People thought she really was an Asian dancer. That made her seem special. In a short time she became a hit in Paris. People from all over Europe came to see her dance. She danced in nothing more than a few thin **veils**. This was her **costume**. She performed in all the big cities of Europe. Rich men gave her money and gifts.

When World War I began in 1914, Mata Hari was 38 years old. Her beauty had faded. By this time, however, she knew many of the most important men in Europe. Men on both the French *and* German sides thought she would make a good spy.

Mata Hari thought so, too. She thought spying would be a great new adventure. She told the French she would work for them. She agreed to gather German secrets. At the same time, however, Mata Hari also took money from the Germans. She told them that she would pass the secrets of France on to them.

Clearly Mata Hari was taking a big chance. Spying for one country is **risky** enough. But being a double agent—a spy who works for both sides—can be deadly. Mata Hari thought it was all just a game. For a couple of years, she played at being a spy. Most of the secrets she passed along were not very important.

Many of Mata Hari's spy games took place at night. She once told a French hotel clerk that she needed walking and exercise in order to fall asleep. She used this excuse to explain why she left the hotel every night to go "for a walk." She said the Paris night life helped her relax. She often did not return until early the next morning.

Mata Hari in full costume

Then, in 1917, the game ended. The Germans sent a message to Mata Hari. The message told her to go to France. There she could pick up the money she had earned for her stolen secrets. Mata Hari went to France to get the money. **Unfortunately** for her, French police knew about this message. They watched her collect her money from a Paris bank. The next day they arrested her.

A Brave Finish

Mata Hari was brought to court in July of 1917. French police charged her with selling secrets to the Germans. They said she had told Germans about the tank. No one knew if this was true. The French police wanted her killed. They said her information had helped Germans build a special gun to be used against the tank. They said her actions had led to the death of at least 50,000 soldiers.

Indonesian temple

Temple dancer today

Mata Hari said she had done nothing wrong. "I was just **pretending** to help the Germans!" she said. "I was really working for France!" Mata Hari told the court that, yes, the Germans had paid her. But that the money was just a gift from some old friends.

No one in the court believed Mata Hari. She was found guilty and **sentenced** to death. Mata Hari faced the news quietly. She told a prison doctor, "Death is nothing. Neither is life. To die is to sleep. What does it really matter? Life is only a dream anyway."

On the morning of October 15, 1917, Mata Hari put on her best clothes and shoes. She was taken from her prison room and led outside. There the firing squad was waiting for her.

A few moments later, the rifles were fired. The most famous spy of World War I was dead.

Building Vocabulary

■ Use the clues to complete the puzzle. Choose from the words in the box.

pass
temple
unfortunately
sentenced
costume
restless
violent
veils
risky
pretending

Across

2. making believe
6. thin pieces of cloth
7. having bad luck
8. kind of church building
9. told how you will be punished

Down

1. using force to harm others
2. get by
3. special clothing
4. dangerous
5. not able to rest

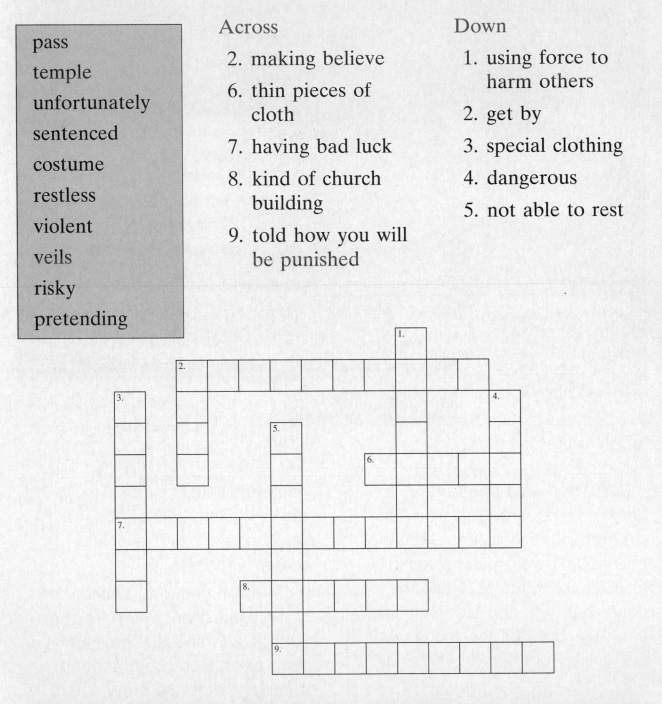

Writing Your Ideas

■ Imagine you worked as a spy with Mata Hari. On a separate sheet of paper, write a short speech you would give to the court.

Remembering What You Read

■ Fill in the circle next to the best ending for each sentence.

1. In the Dutch West Indies, Margaretha watched
   ○ a. airplanes.　　　○ b. island dancers.　　　○ c. spies.

2. Mata Hari was charged with selling secrets about
   ○ a. Paris banks.　　　○ b. her father.　　　○ c. the tank.

3. Mata Hari told the court that she had done
   ○ a. nothing wrong.　　　○ b. terrible things.　　　○ c. no dancing.

4. Mata Hari was
   ○ a. put to death.　　　○ b. sent to Russia.　　　○ c. honored.

Thinking Critically—Cause and Effect

■ Complete the following sentences.

1. Margaretha Zelle got married at age 18 because _____

   _____

   _____

2. Margaretha pretended to be an Asian dancer because _____

   _____

   _____

3. Mata Hari agreed to gather war secrets because _____

   _____

   _____

4. The French police wanted Mata Hari killed because _____

   _____

5. Mata Hari was not upset about being sentenced to death

   because _____

   _____

65

RED BARON SHOT DOWN!

April 21, 1918—The "Red Baron" of Germany will fly no more. The Red Baron—Baron Manfred von Richthofen—was shot down and killed today near Amiens, France. He was struck down by British fighters and ground guns firing on him from all sides. This man had shot down 80 enemy planes. With the death of the Red Baron, Germany loses its top fighter pilot.

The Making of a Fighter Pilot

Baron Manfred von Richthofen was born in Germany on May 2, 1892. From the beginning his father wanted him to be a soldier. So at just 11 years old, the Baron was sent to an army school. There he learned to be a soldier.

When he finished school in 1911, von Richthofen became an army officer. He led a **cavalry** on horses. Three years later World War I broke out. The Germans found themselves fighting the Russians, French, and British.

Baron von Richthofen was sent to the Russian front. There he discovered that men on horses couldn't fight in modern wars.

The young Baron wanted to be in the fighting. So he asked for a **post** in France. He wanted to join an **infantry** there. He was sent to France. But von Richthofen did not get a battle post. He got the lowly job of collecting food. Baron von Richthofen was angry. He wanted a more important job. He wrote to the officer in charge, "I have not gone to war to collect cheese and eggs."

The Red Baron in his plane

A German Fokker DR-1 like the one the Red Baron flew

In May of 1915, the young officer finally got the job he wanted. He joined the German air force. But the first time the Baron flew a plane, he crashed. Slowly, however, his flying skills improved. By March 1916, von Richthofen was good enough to become a fighter pilot. The Baron **insisted** that every plane he flew be painted red. This soon earned him the name "Red Baron." Later, people would say that the name fit him well for another reason. It was a symbol of all the enemy blood he spilled.

Dogfights and Trophies

On September 17, 1916, the Red Baron shot a British plane out of the sky. It was the first time he had killed anyone. The Red Baron bought himself a small silver **trophy** cup to mark the kill. Over the next two years, von Richthofen added 79 more cups to his collection.

By November 1916, the Red Baron led his own group of pilots. They traveled the skies looking for air fights. Such fights were called dogfights. Fighting planes would turn and **whirl**, like dogs trying to bite each other's tail. The winner was the pilot who could stay above and behind his enemy. From there he could shoot down the enemy plane.

On November 23, 1916, the Red Baron was flying the skies as usual. He was looking for his 11th kill. He ended up in a dogfight with Lanoe Hawker, Britain's best fighter pilot. After a long and bitter battle, the Red Baron hit Hawker from behind. Hawker's plane crashed to the ground. The Red Baron became even more **confident**. "No one can stop me now," he thought.

The Red Baron and other pilots at the airfield

69

erfolgreichsten

The Red Baron, his brother, and three other officers

After killing Hawker the Red Baron became famous. The German people loved him. He was their hero. The British knew him as a dangerous enemy. British pilots tried to shoot him down. But in dogfight after dogfight, it was the Red Baron who came out alive.

On April 20, 1918, the Red Baron shot down two more British pilots—his 79th and 80th. A German band greeted the Red Baron as he landed back home. The band played to honor their hero. The next day it was the Red Baron's turn to be a **casualty**.

The Final Battle

The sky was bright and clear on that Sunday morning. At the airport a German **mechanic** came running up to von Richthofen. "Please," he begged, "may I take a picture of you standing next to your plane?"

"Okay," snapped von Richthofen. "But make it quick. Pictures before a flight can bring bad luck."

After the picture the Red Baron took off to attack two British planes. Five German pilots joined him. As the battle began, other British pilots saw flashes of smoke in the air. They knew what the smoke meant—British planes were under attack! A group of pilots, led by Captain Arthur Brown, flew to help their friends.

Captain Brown waved to his men to be careful. Brown was **especially** concerned about pilot Wilfred May. This was May's first flight as a fighter. "Stay out of the fight," Brown had told May before they started out that morning. "You can watch and learn, but stay out of the fight."

May, however, got too close. The Red Baron spotted him and moved in for the kill. The young May saw the red plane diving down on him. Quickly May turned and headed back toward the British base. The Red Baron followed, hot on his tail.

Brown was in a dogfight with one of the Germans when he saw that May was in trouble. Brown broke away from his fight and raced after the Red Baron. The three planes flew at high speed over the tops of the trees. Captain Brown opened fire on the Red Baron. So, too, did soldiers on the ground. Suddenly, the Baron's red plane crashed to the ground. A bullet had hit von Richthofen in the heart. The Red Baron of Germany was dead.

Portrait of the Red Baron a year before he died

Building Vocabulary

Part A

■ Write the best word to complete each sentence. Use each word once.

insisted	casualty	confident	trophy

The Red Baron (1)_____ that he fly in red planes. He

gave himself a (2)_____ for every enemy pilot he killed.

He felt (3)_____ that he would never lose an air battle.

But at last he, too, became a (4)_____ of the war.

Part B

■ Match each word with its meaning.

_____ 1. cavalry   a. someone who fixes machines

_____ 2. especially   b. group of soldiers on horseback

_____ 3. post   c. turn around quickly

_____ 4. infantry   d. more than usual

_____ 5. mechanic   e. group of soldiers on foot

_____ 6. whirl   f. place where a soldier
                             does his or her job

Writing Your Ideas

■ Imagine you are a young British pilot. On a separate sheet of
paper, describe your feelings about living through a dogfight with
the Red Baron.

Remembering What You Read

■ Answer the questions.

1. Why was Baron von Richthofen angry when he was given the job of collecting food? _____

_____

2. Why was Richthofen called the Red Baron? _____

_____

3. How did the German people feel about the Red Baron? _____

_____

4. Why did Captain Brown want May to stay away from the Red Baron? _____

Building Skills—Use a Map

■ Use the map of Germany to answer the questions.

1. Name three rivers that flow through Germany.

_____

_____

_____

2. Circle four German cities on the map.

3. What two cities are capital cities? _____

_____

_____

4. What two seas border Germany? _____

_____

Modern Germany

⊙ Capital City
• Other City
– Border Between Countries

North Sea
Baltic Sea
Hamburg
Berlin ⊙
Elbe River
Ruhr River
Bonn ⊙
Rhine River
Danube River
Munich

N W E S

0   100
Miles

NIGHTMARE IN BOSTON!

September 10, 1919—There is trouble in Boston, Massachusetts. At 5:00 P.M. yesterday, Boston police officers walked off the job. They say they won't come back to work until city leaders agree to be fair to them. With no police on the streets, criminals are running wild. Last night gangs broke into stores. People were robbed. Many were beaten. Tonight might be even worse. Criminals from all over the state are heading to Boston to join the attacks.

Soldiers guard stores after the riots.

A Long, Hard Summer

The summer of 1919 was not an easy one for the Boston police. The days were long and hot. Police officers were tired. They had to work 12 hours every day. Their offices were dirty and small. Police stations were so crowded that the officers could hardly move. The men were not well paid for their work. They even had to buy their own uniforms!

To many officers the answer to their problems seemed clear. They should form a workers' **union**. No one police officer had the power to change working **conditions**. But together, the officers could make changes happen. As a union, the police could demand better working conditions.

This was not a new idea. Police in 37 other cities had formed unions. In Boston, however, it would not be easy to do. The police **commissioner** hated unions. His name was Edwin Curtis. Curtis told his men that they could not join a union. He made a rule that they could not join *any* club or group.

The officers thought this was crazy. They went ahead with their plans. On August 11, 1919, they formed the Boston Police Union. This made Curtis angry. He put 19 union leaders on police **trial** for breaking his rule. All were found guilty.

The Police Walk Out

Police around the city complained loudly. "Curtis has pushed us around too long!" they cried. Many talked about a **strike**. "We should just walk off the job! We should stay out on strike until Curtis starts being fair with us!"

Curtis knew how the men felt. Still, he refused to change his mind. He told police officers they could not go on strike. He said they had a **duty** to protect the people of Boston. "If you strike you will be walking away from your duty," he said. "You have no right to do that!" On Monday, September 8, Curtis **suspended** the 19 union leaders. This was too much for the other officers to stand. The Boston Police Union took a vote. Over 1,100 officers voted to strike. Only two officers voted against the idea.

A soldier acts as a police officer during the police strike.

State troops are called in.

At 5:00 P.M. on Tuesday, the police walked out of their station houses. They were still wearing their uniforms. But they had taken off their badges. The police force was no longer going to keep the peace. Suddenly the people of Boston were on their own. They could not count on the police for any help.

Not much happened at first. But as the night wore on, things became wild. People knew that no one was around to keep law and order. Criminals took over the streets. They threw rocks at the empty police stations. They broke into stores. Goods worth $60,000 were scattered in the streets.

By Wednesday morning the people of Boston didn't know what to do. Firefighters and other city workers supported the strike. Some talked about leaving their own jobs and joining the striking officers. Bankers and store owners, on the other hand, spoke out against the strike. They didn't want their businesses destroyed by gangs of criminals. Some owners locked their shops. They stood inside with loaded guns. They promised to shoot anyone who broke in.

By Wednesday evening criminals from outside Boston had arrived in the city. They came to cause trouble. **Riots** broke out. People were **assaulted**. The crowd became more violent than the night before. Criminals threw bricks, stones, and bottles at anyone who tried to stop them. Soon the night turned bloody. Shots were fired in downtown Boston. People were killed all over the city. On Thursday morning Boston papers shouted the news: Riots and **Bloodshed** in City! Boston was out of control.

The Nightmare Ends

At last government leaders stepped in. The Governor of Massachusetts was Calvin Coolidge. Coolidge knew what had been happening. But he had stayed out of it. He wanted the police commissioner and the mayor to handle the problem. Besides, Coolidge agreed with Curtis. He didn't think the police had a right to strike. Coolidge said, "There is no right to strike against the public safety by anybody, any time, anywhere!"

Governor Coolidge with soldiers

Police Commissioner Edwin Curtis

Coolidge later became the 30th President of the U.S.

By Thursday, however, Coolidge had to act. The people of Boston needed help. Coolidge called for the State Guard to protect the city. He also announced that he was taking control of the Boston police force.

The people of Boston cheered these moves. They wanted peace in their city. The striking officers saw that the public no longer supported them. The officers quickly voted to end their strike. It was too late, however. Coolidge and Curtis made plans to hire and train new officers. None of the strikers were ever allowed to return to police work.

Calvin Coolidge became a hero for ending the strike. People saw him as a man who stood for law and order. It later helped him gain the job of President of the United States.

Building Vocabulary

Part A

■ Match each word with its meaning.

_____ 1. suspended   a. attacked

_____ 2. trial   b. a court hearing to decide if a crime has been committed

_____ 3. duty   c. taken off the job

_____ 4. assaulted   d. the way things are

_____ 5. bloodshed   e. the loss of blood or death

_____ 6. conditions   f. what you are supposed to do

Part B

■ Write the best word to complete each sentence. Use each word once.

| commissioner | union | riots | strike |

In 1919 Boston police tried to form a (1)_____. The

police (2)_____ punished 19 union leaders. Police across

the city then went on (3)_____. Soon Boston was torn

apart by (4)_____.

Writing Your Ideas

■ Imagine you are a citizen of Boston. On a separate sheet of paper, tell whether you support the police strike and why.

Remembering What You Read

■ Fill in the circle next to the best ending for each sentence.

1. In the summer of 1919, the Boston police were
   ○ a. getting rich.   ○ b. given a pay raise.
   ○ c. unhappy over how they were treated.

2. The Boston police commissioner hated
   ○ a. Governor Coolidge.   ○ b. unions.
   ○ c. bankers and shopkeepers.

3. When the police went on strike, criminals
   ○ a. went into hiding.   ○ b. rushed to join the riots.
   ○ c. tried to become city workers.

4. Calvin Coolidge became a
   ○ a. hero.   ○ b. criminal.   ○ c. police officer.

Thinking Critically—Sequence

■ Number the sentences to show the order in which things happened in the story. The first one is done for you.

_____ The Boston Police Union voted to go on strike.

_____ Store owners stood inside their shops with loaded guns.

_____ Calvin Coolidge called for the State Guard's help.

__1__ Police in 37 cities formed unions.

_____ Commissioner Curtis suspended 19 union leaders.

_____ The Boston police were unhappy with how they were treated.

EMMA GOLDMAN SENT BACK TO RUSSIA

December 21, 1919—The *Buford* will set sail out of New York Harbor today. Passengers on board were ordered to leave the country and never return. They are men and women considered troublemakers by the U.S. government. Among them is Emma Goldman—once called the most dangerous woman in the world. For years Goldman has spoken out against the rich and powerful. In a few weeks, Goldman will set foot on Russian soil, where she was born fifty years ago.

Coming to America

As a young girl in Russia, Emma was **miserable**. When she was 15, her father picked out a husband for her. Emma refused to marry the man. "If you make me marry this man," Emma cried, "I'll jump in the Neva River and drown myself!"

Emma's father finally backed down. But by then she had decided to move far away. Later that year Emma and an older sister **emigrated** to the United States. They arrived in December 1885 and settled in Rochester, New York.

Fighting for Change

For Emma, life in the United States did not seem much better than life in Russia. She got a job in a New York clothing factory. She worked ten and a half hours a day, six days a week. Her pay was $2.50 a week. She **criticized** the factory owners who did not treat workers fairly.

Emma Goldman, fighter for the poor

Emma speaks in New York City in 1916.

Then on November 11, 1887, four Chicago men were hanged. These men held a peaceful **rally** for workers' rights. Near the end of the rally, a bomb was thrown. Eleven people were killed. No one knew who threw the bomb. Although there was no proof, rally leaders were blamed. After a trial, four of the eight rally leaders were hanged. This was a turning point for Emma. She felt "too **horrible** even for tears."

Emma felt that **injustices** such as this had to be stopped. She began meeting with other young people who agreed with her. Emma and her friends spoke out against the government. They believed that the government only protected the rights of the **wealthy**. Emma found she was a gifted speaker. "Only when all people share power equally will things be fair," she said.

In 1893 Emma was sent to jail for a year. What was her crime? She had given a speech to people who didn't have jobs. She told them it was their right to steal bread if they needed it to feed their families.

Back to Russia

After she got out of jail, Emma went back to public speaking. Workers and students gathered to hear her speak. So did the police. They kept a close eye on this woman with the "dangerous" ideas against the government. In fact, in 1908 the United States took back her citizenship.

In 1917 the United States began **drafting** men to fight in World War I. Emma was against the war and wanted to stop the draft. She wrote papers and gave speeches against the war. In June police arrested her. They charged her with hurting the war **effort**. She was sent back to jail for two more years.

When Emma was freed in 1919, the government didn't want to take any chances. She was **deported** for her dangerous acts against the government. Emma left peacefully. But she didn't give up her beliefs. She took her fight to many other countries. She hoped to make life better for all people who were being treated unfairly. Emma died in 1940.

Emma Goldman and her friend Alexander Berkman, shortly before they are deported

Building Vocabulary

■ To complete the sentences choose a word from the box. Write the word on the blanks after the sentence. The letters in the boxes will spell the answer to question 10.

effort	horrible	injustices	emigrated	deported
rally	drafting	wealthy	criticized	

1. Emma _____ to America.
   ☐ _ _ _ _ _ _ _ _

2. Emma _____ factory owners.
   _ _ _ ☐ _ _ _ _ _

3. Emma saw many _____ in America.
   _ _ _ ☐ _ _ _ _ _

4. Emma fought against the _____.
   _ _ _ ☐ _ _ _ _

5. Emma was _____ to Russia.
   _ _ _ _ ☐ _ _ _

6. In 1917, the U.S. began _____ men.
   _ _ _ ☐ _ _ _ _ _

7. Emma felt _____ after the hanging.
   _ _ _ _ _ ☐ _ _

8. Workers held a peaceful _____ in Chicago.
   _ _ ☐ _ _

9. People said Emma hurt the war _____.
   ☐ _ _ _ _ _

10. What were Emma's early years in Russia like?_____

Writing Your Ideas

■ Imagine you are Emma Goldman. On a separate sheet of paper, write a journal entry. Describe how you feel about being deported.

Remembering What You Read

■ Some of the statements below are true. Others are false. Place a check in front of the three things that happened in the story.

_____ 1. Emma Goldman refused to marry the man her father had picked out.

_____ 2. Emma Goldman became a factory worker in America.

_____ 3. Emma Goldman was a soldier in World War I.

_____ 4. Emma Goldman's husband was hanged in Chicago.

_____ 5. Emma Goldman believed all people should share power equally.

_____ 6. Emma Goldman became a leader in the U.S. government.

Building Skills—Use a Time Line

■ Use the time line to answer the questions.

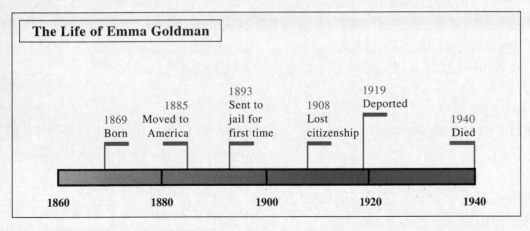

The Life of Emma Goldman

1869 Born
1885 Moved to America
1893 Sent to jail for first time
1908 Lost citizenship
1919 Deported
1940 Died

1860   1880   1900   1920   1940

1. What year was Emma Goldman born?_____

2. Was Emma Goldman still a U.S. citizen when she was deported?

_____

3. When did Emma first go to jail?_____

_____

4. Mark and label the time line to show when the four Chicago rally leaders were hanged.

Glossary

admired, page 25
To admire something is to think highly of it.

arose, page 35
Arose means appeared.

arrests, page 41
An arrest is when the police hold a person in jail. Police arrest someone when they believe he or she has done something that is against the law.

articles, page 55
Articles are stories and reports written for newspapers or magazines.

assaulted, page 78
To be assaulted is to be attacked by someone who wants to hurt you.

astronomers, page 11
Astronomers are people who study stars.

attention, page 5
To pay attention is to watch, listen, or think about something.

bloodshed, page 78
Bloodshed means the loss of blood or death. World War I caused much bloodshed.

bomb, page 41
A bomb is a weapon that causes harm by bursting apart.

bother, page 48
To bother with something is to take the time and trouble to do it. Don't bother to visit her, she doesn't want to see anyone.

brightness, page 13
Brightness means how much light something gives.

Bureau of Indian Affairs, page 54
The Bureau of Indian Affairs is a government office set up to help Native Americans.

calm, page 39
When someone calms down, he or she becomes quieter and more peaceful.

casualty, page 70
A casualty is someone who is hurt or killed in a war.

cavalry, page 67
A cavalry is a group of soldiers trained to fight on horseback.

citizenship, page 55
Citizenship means being a member of a country. A citizen enjoys all the rights that other people in that country have.

claimed, page 28
To claim something is to say that it is true.

class, page 15
A class is a group of things that are alike in some way.

clues, page 28
Clues are hints.

college, page 35
College is a school of higher learning.

commissioner, page 75
A commissioner is the person in charge of a government department.

committee, page 35
A committee is a group of people who work together to make decisions.

concerned, page 55
To be concerned is to be worried.

conditions, page 75
Conditions mean the way things are. Working conditions include the hours, safety, and comfort of a work place.

confident, page 69
To be confident is to feel sure of yourself.

continent, page 47
A continent is one of the seven large land areas in the world. The seven continents are North America, South America, Europe, Africa, Asia, Australia, and Antarctica.

costume, page 60
A costume is the special clothing a person wears while performing a dance or play.

courage, page 41
Courage means being brave.

crime, page 27
A crime is an action that breaks the law.

criticized, page 83
To criticize means to say what is bad about something.

declared, page 43
To declare is to announce or say something openly.

deported, page 85
To be deported means to be forced to leave a country.

determined, page 6
To be determined means to try hard without giving up.

disaster, page 19
A disaster is a happening that causes great suffering.

discouraged, page 55
To be discouraged is to lose hope.

drafting, page 85
To draft means to call a person to war. Many young men were drafted during World War II.

duty, page 76
A duty is something you are supposed to do. One of her duties was to lock up the shop.

education, page 53
To have an education means to have learned in school and from life.

effort, page 85

Effort means work. The war effort was the work people did to win the war.

emigrated, page 83

To emigrate means to leave the country you were born in and move to another country.

emperor, page 39

An emperor is the king or ruler of a group of countries.

endangered, page 48

If a group of animals is endangered, it is close to dying out. Many people are now trying to protect endangered animals.

enrolled, page 53

To enroll means to sign up to join a class or group.

especially, page 71

Especially means extra or more than usual. I was especially worried about my science grade.

events, page 34

An event is a sports contest. He won two swimming events.

exact, page 13

Exact means completely right.

exploded, page 42

To explode means to burst apart suddenly.

famous, page 5

To be famous is to be well known.

flocks, page 47

Flocks are groups of birds that travel together. Groups of sheep are also called flocks.

glided, page 7

To glide is to move smoothly. See the skater glide across the ice.

graduated, page 54

To graduate means to finish studying at a school.

gravel, page 19

Gravel is small bits of rock. Gravel is used to make roads.

haze, page 19

Haze is dust in the air.

honest, page 35

Honest means real and true.

horrible, page 84

Horrible means terrible.

horrified, page 27

To be horrified is to be very angry and upset.

impulse, page 33

An impulse is a sudden feeling to act without thinking or planning.

infantry, page 67

An infantry is a group of soldiers trained to fight on foot.

injured, page 42

If someone is injured, he or she is hurt.

injustices, page 84

Injustices are things that are not fair.

insisted, page 68

To insist is to say that something must be done.

jab, page 7

A jab is a quick punch.

laps, page 21

A lap is one trip around a track.

limestone, page 19

Limestone is a kind of hard rock often used for building.

mechanic, page 70

A mechanic is a person who fixes motors and other machines.

miserable, page 83

Miserable means very unhappy.

mysteriously, page 25

A mysterious event is one that is hard to explain.

novas, page 15

Novas are stars that suddenly become very bright—then fade over time.

observatory, page 11

An observatory is a building with equipment for studying the stars.

organized, page 12

To be organized is to keep things in order.

outrageous, page 42

Outrageous means shocking and hard to believe.

oval, page 19

Oval means shaped like an egg.

pass, page 60

To pass means to get by. If you pass for a German, it means people believe you are German.

paved, page 20

To pave is to cover a street with a hard surface.

photographers, page 26

Photographers are people who take pictures.

position, page 12

The position of something is where it is.

post, page 67

A post is in a certain place where a soldier does his or her job.

potential, page 33

Potential is what a person is able to do. She has the potential to be a wonderful student.

powerful, page 7

Powerful means strong.

practiced, page 49

To practice is to do something again and again in order to become good at it.

pretending, page 63

To pretend means to make believe.

proved, page 7

To prove something means to show it is true.

rally, page 84

A rally is a meeting held for a reason. During a rally people sometimes march through the streets holding signs.

recognize, page 26

If you recognize something you remember it from the past.

reservations, page 54

A reservation is a piece of land the government set aside for Native Americans to live on and use.

restless, page 59

Restless means not able to rest.

retired, page 6

To retire is to stop taking part in a job or activity. He retired after teaching for 20 years.

riots, page 78

A riot is when a group of people become angry and act rough. During riots people often destroy things and hurt or kill others.

risky, page 60

Something that is risky is dangerous.

rot, page 49

To rot is to become spoiled. If you don't eat the peaches soon, they will rot.

royal, page 40

Royal means having to do with a king or queen. The royal palace was huge.

sentenced, page 63

To be sentenced is to be told by a court how you will be punished for a crime.

seriously, page 6

To take something seriously means not to joke about it.

settlers, page 48

Settlers are people who move into new lands and make their homes there.

shattered, page 35

To shatter is to destroy.

slammed, page 21

To slam is to hit hard.

species, page 47

A species is a group of animals that are the same type of animal. Robins and eagles are different species of birds.

spectacular, page 20

Spectacular means wonderful.

sport, page 49

To do something for sport is to make a game out of it.

strike, page 76

A strike is when workers refuse to work. The workers went on strike to get better pay and shorter hours.

struggled, page 19

To struggle is to work very hard.

survived, page 49
To survive is to stay alive or live through something dangerous.

suspended, page 76
To suspend workers is to take them off the job for a period of time.

system, page 15
A system is a way of doing something.

temple, page 60
A temple is a kind of church building.

title, page 5
A title is the name given to a sports champion.

touchdowns, page 34
A touchdown is the scoring of six points in a football game.

treasures, page 25
Treasures are things that are important and valuable.

treatment, page 55
Treatment means the way people act toward others.

trial, page 76
A trial is when facts are presented in a court of law to decide whether or not a person is guilty of a crime.

tribal, page 33
Tribal means something that has to do with a tribe or group of Native Americans. The tribal dances were beautiful to watch.

trophy, page 68
A trophy is a cup or statue given to honor someone who has done something special.

unfortunately, page 62
Unfortunately means having bad luck.

union, page 75
A union is a group of workers who join together to fight for their rights.

variable, page 15
Variable means likely to change. A variable star shines brightly some times and not so brightly other times.

veils, page 60
Veils are light, thin pieces of cloth.

violent, page 59
If someone is violent, he or she uses force to harm others.

wealthy, page 84
Wealthy means rich. The wealthy family had two large homes.

whirl, page 69
To whirl means to turn around quickly.

works, page 25
Works are pieces of art.

Keeping Score

1. Count the number of correct answers you have for each activity.
2. Write these numbers in the boxes in the chart.
3. Ask your teacher to give you a score (maximum score 5) for Writing Your Ideas.
4. Add up the numbers to get a final score.

Stories	Building Vocabulary	Writing Your Ideas	Remembering What You Read	Building Skills	Thinking Critically	Score
Fight of the Century						/21
New Star Discovered						/21
Speedway Spectacular!						/27
Mona Lisa Stolen!						/22
Jim Thorpe Captures Gold!						/23
Archduke Ferdinand Shot						/22
Last Passenger Pigeon Dies						/21
Let My People Go!						/23
Mata Hari Arrested!						/24
Red Baron Shot Down!						/29
Nightmare in Boston!						/24
Emma Goldman Sent Back to Russia						/22

Answer Key

The Fight of the Century   Pages 4–9

Building Vocabulary
Part A: 1. title, 2. retired,
3. powerful, 4. proved
Part B: 1-e, 2-a, 3-b, 4-f, 5-d, 6-c

Writing Your Ideas Answers will vary.

Remembering What You Read
1. They didn't want an African American to be champion.
2. He was a farmer and had gained weight.
3. He ran, skipped rope, and boxed.
4. Johnson knocked out Jeffries in the 15th round.

Thinking Critically—Main Ideas
1, 4

New Star Discovered   Pages 10–17

Building Vocabulary
Across: 1. position, 5. astronomers,
8. variable, 9. system, 10. brightness
Down: 2. observatory, 3. organized,
4. nova, 6. exact, 7. class

Writing Your Ideas Answers will vary.

Remembering What You Read
2, 4, 5

Building Skills—Use A Diagram
1. The first step is to photograph the stars.
2. Finding the position of a star is done before measuring its brightness.
3. The last step, develop new classes of stars, is not always needed.

Speedway Spectacular   Pages 18–23

Building Vocabulary
1-a, 2-c, 3-b, 4-a, 5-c, 6-a, 7-c, 8-c, 9-b, 10-b

Writing Your Ideas Answers will vary.

Remembering What You Read
1. He hoped Indianapolis would become the auto center of America.
2. He wanted to hold long races without raising lots of dust and causing accidents.
3. He wanted to race alone and he needed to be able to see behind him.

4. The drivers had to face accidents, crashes, and oil on the track.

Thinking Critically—Fact or Opinion
1-O, 2-F, 3-O, 4-F, 5-F, 6-O, 7-F, 8-O

Mona Lisa Stolen   Pages 24–31

Building Vocabulary
1. mysteriously, 2. crime, 3. recognize,
4. admired, 5. works, 6. clues, 7. horrified,
8. claimed, 9. photographers
CODE WORD: TREASURES

Writing Your Ideas Answers will vary.

Remembering What You Read
1-b, 2-a, 3-c, 4-b

Building Skills—Read a Table
1. a woman (Lisa del Gioconda)
2. It was painted in 1510-1511.
3. Michelangelo painted it.

Jim Thorpe Captures Gold!   Pages 32–37

Building Vocabulary
1. impulse, 2. honest, 3. arose, 4. events,
5. potential, 6. committee, 7. tribal,
8. college, 9. touchdowns
10. CODE WORD: SHATTERED

Writing Your Ideas Answers will vary.

Remembering What You Read
1-c, 2-a, 3-b, 4-b

Thinking Critically—Conclusions
1. he had no one to take care of him.
2. he had earned money playing baseball.
3. his gold medals were taken away.
4. the Olympic Committee decided they had made a mistake.

Archduke Ferdinand Shot   Pages 38–45

Building Vocabulary
Part A: 1-e, 2-g, 3-b, 4-f, 5-a, 6-d, 7-c
Part B: 1. bomb, 2. injured, 3. declared

Writing Your Ideas Answers will vary.

Remembering What You Read
2, 3, 6

Building Skills—Read a Graph
1. 53,513   2. 204,002

3. More died in other ways.

Last Passenger Pigeon Dies   Pages 46–51

Building Vocabulary
1-b, 2-a, 3-b, 4-a, 5-b, 6-a, 7-c, 8-b, 9-a, 10-c

Writing Your Ideas Answers will vary.

Remembering What You Read
1. The birds "passed" from place to place.
2. Native Americans never killed more pigeons than they could eat and never killed any when young birds were feeding.
3. Passenger pigeons died out because large numbers were killed for sport and for food.
4. Martha was the last passenger pigeon.

Thinking Critically—Main Ideas
3, 5

Let My People Go!   Pages 52–57

Building Vocabulary
Part A: 1-b, 2-b, 3-b, 4-a
Part B: 1-d, 2-c, 3-f, 4-a, 5-e, 6-b

Writing Your Ideas Answers will vary.

Remembering What You Read
2, 3, 4

Building Skills—Use a Time Line
1. He was captured by the Pima Indians.
2. Society of American Indians
3. 1883   4. 1923
5. Montezuma quit the Bureau in 1897. (Students should mark this on time line.)

Mata Hari Arrested!   Pages 58–65

Building Vocabulary
Across: 2. pretending, 6. veils, 7. unfortunately, 8. temple, 9. sentenced
Down: 1. violent, 2. pass, 3. costume, 4. risky, 5. restless

Writing Your Ideas Answers will vary.

Remembering What You Read
1-b, 2-c, 3-a, 4-a

Thinking Critically—Cause and Effect
1. she wanted to get away from home.
2. it was a way to get work as a dancer.
3. she wanted a new adventure.
4. they believed she had told the Germans

about the tank.
5. she thought death would be like sleep.

Red Baron Shot Down!   Pages 66–73

Building Vocabulary
Part A: 1. insisted, 2. trophy, 3. confident, 4. casualty
Part B: 1-b, 2-d, 3-f, 4-e, 5-a, 6-c

Writing Your Ideas Answers will vary.

Remembering What You Read
1. He wanted a more important job.
2. He flew red planes and spilled a lot of enemy blood.
3. They loved him and felt he was a hero.
4. It was May's first dogfight.

Building Skills—Use a Map
1. Answers may include Rhine River, Ruhr River, Elbe River, and Danube River.
2. Answers may include Berlin, Bonn, Munich, and Hamburg.
3. Berlin and Bonn
4. North Sea and Baltic Sea

Nightmare in Boston!   Pages 74–81

Building Vocabulary
Part A: 1-c, 2-b, 3-f, 4-a, 5-e, 6-d
Part B: 1. union, 2. commissioner, 3. strike, 4. riots

Writing Your Ideas Answers will vary.

Remembering What You Read
1-c, 2-b, 3-b, 4-a

Thinking Critically—Sequence
4, 5, 6, 1, 3, 2

Emma Goldman Sent Back to Russia   Pages 82–87

Building Vocabulary
1. emigrated, 2. criticized, 3. injustices, 4. wealthy, 5. deported, 6. drafting, 7. horrible, 8. rally, 9. effort
10. CODE WORD: MISERABLE

Writing Your Ideas Answers will vary.

Remembering What You Read
1, 2, 5

Building Skills—Use a Time Line
1. 1869 2. no 3. 1893
4. Rally leaders were hanged in 1887.